BIG MIND

small mind

Other books by David Mugun

Tearless Living. 2011

10 Critical Success Answers for SMEs. 2012

Rock Solid in All Seasons. 2017

Brave Cowards. 2018

BIG MIND
small mind.

David Mugun

Published by

THE SCRIBE CENTRE
We are empowering the world

P.O. Box 35-00621, Nairobi, Kenya

April 2019 © David Mugun,

First published, April 2019

Contents

DEDICATION

This is to the people crossing over to big mind territory and all big minds out there.

ACKNOWLEDGEMENTS

To Almighty God for seeing me through with my 5th book.

To all who have in one way or another aided in the writing of this book. I cannot list everyone by name but please accept my acknowledgment.

INTRODUCTION

Big mind small mind is a simple read with huge implications.

Enjoy reading.

Chapter 1 Understanding Big mind Small mind concept - BMsm

Ever heard the saying that "small minds discuss people, average minds discuss events, but great minds discuss ideas."? And on that note, someone said, "Show me your friends, and I will tell you who you are." They may then rank you as a small, average or a big mind.

There is also my favourite one. "In every man's head, there is always a foolish corner." All these sayings point us to ourselves. We are a bit of both big and small minds. What differentiates us all is the degree or intensity of either mind.

Big Mind small mind-BMsm, acknowledges that everyone alive today has in them a big side and a small side. That is the reason why a man acclaimed by many as great, can sometimes act in a manner that attracts comments such as "unbelievable" or "He has gotten the shine off his hitherto impeccable character."

At this early moment, I wish to introduce a concept first used by Eckhart Tolle, the author of "The Power of Now." The term "Painbody".

It is an accumulation of a painful life experience that was not fully faced and accepted at the moment it arose. It leaves behind an energy form of emotional pain.

It comes together with other energy forms from other instances, and so after some years, you have a "painbody," an energy entity consisting of old emotion. Painbody solicitation and nourishment are the small mind's specialty. It may stay dormant for a while but it surely erupts during some heavy emotional moments.

I liken it to anthrax, the deadly bacterial disease. Underneath the calm waters of a lake, these microbes may lay dormant and will not affect the hippopotami that swim its length and breadth.

However, when the waters recede during a biting drought, the animals scramble for space in the dwindling waters and in the process, stir up anthrax-causing bacteria that lay at the bottom of the lake.

In some national parks, hippopotami have fallen victims in the wrathful wake of these microbes. All was peaceful when there was enough for everyone. Coincidentally, the small mind wastefully thrives in scarcity.

But painbody is a separate concept from the other attribute of a small mind. Conniving tendencies dominate the small mind for whatever reasons may aid it to achieve the desired end.

The big mind focuses on beneficial matters such as long term plans, positive living, building alliances and spreading out the love to others. In short, it is a profitable attitude.

The small mind is the exact opposite. It is about short term gains, selfish attitudes, ungrateful ideas, hurting others and possibly self in the process. It is a loss-making attitude.

BMsm does not discriminate on anyone. Be it, a parent, child, boss or spiritual leader, BMsm is at play.

Let us get to understand BMsm better through the story below.

Three colleagues, Andrew, Bernard, and Carlton work under Donald the Finance Division Vice President at EFG Incorporated. All three are on equal footing and two job grades below Donald.

The joke in the company whenever they hold a departmental meeting is about the first letter in their names. They say ABCD is meeting EFG and because alphabetically the first seven letters are involved, they are collectively referred to as the G7.

Andrew made his mark when the economy was in recession. The company was facing a bad cash crunch and his initiatives saw them through when most competitors scaled down significantly or closed shop. For this lifeline giving efforts, Andrew is popular in the senior management circles.

Bernard made an indelible mark on the shareholders with his accurate analyses of the state of the business.

When the company wanted to decide on management's proposal to buy out a struggling competitor with strengths where EFG Inc. needed growth so badly, Bernard came in handy.

The decision to go ahead with the purchase got EFG Inc. to the number one slot in market share within a year.

Carlton is a genius of a different kind. Whenever a crisis that bears a huge reputational risk on the company arises, and there have been many over the last three years, he is the official Mr. Fix it.

Most recently, Carlton led the negotiations with the authorities that saw EFG Inc. get further licenses to deal in additional product lines despite inspection reports revealing some breaches in meeting set standards.

When the staff union pushed had for wage increments because of discrepancies brought about by the variations in pay, between the original staff and those inherited from the purchased competitor, Carlton fixed things to everyone's satisfaction. Carlton is very popular with the staff union members.

Owing to the much bigger entity after the merger, a need to have someone to deputize Donald has arisen.

It has not been announced officially but they all have their hands on the company's pulse and the information has reached every one of them individually.

The company's policy to promote from within is what all three chaps are banking on and everyone has stepped up their efforts to get Donald's endorsement for the job.

An announcement is imminent and Donald calls the three guys to a meeting in the boardroom. He informs them that the new position will go to one of them. Donald expects whoever is not picked to give his full support to his new deputy. The President will make the announcement upon his return from a two weeks visit overseas.

Everyone's excitement at the prospects of the promotion is short lived. The possibility of not being the one dawns on them and as it sinks in, every one of them gets busy scheming.

Andrew conspires with close colleagues to expose Bernard and Carlton's largesse lifestyles on company money over the last three business trips. These get picked in the internal audit report that was emailed out to management for discussion the following week.

Bernard works with other business analysts. The official report to management captures disturbing inconsistencies in the amounts of money spent by EFG Inc. on staff wages as it clearly showed that those from Andrew's and Carlton's home counties benefited the most and were the highest earners in the rank and file.

Carlton works his underhand plans with the union officials. The union leader writes to management confirming that they are aware of the upcoming announcement to promote either Andrew or Bernard.

He makes it clear that such plans are not welcome because the two are the cause of disharmony within the ranks and will not receive any cooperation from union members. Go-slows or strikes are an expensive affair.

A week to the President's return, two online recruitment sites advertised the vacancy at EFG Inc. and therein, it is made clear that internal staff need not apply. The closing date was within a two weeks period.

At the weekly meeting with Donald, the three jilted contenders for the deputy's position raised the issue.

And Donald cleverly informed them that at the senior management meeting to review the situation; it became apparent that replacing any one of them in the event of the promotion proved hard because none of them had a clear succession plan for those working below them.

Donald now made it a key deliverable for all three to submit clear succession plans within two weeks.

Within a month of the President's return from overseas, Donald had a new deputy, Harry, from outside the company. Harry now made it G8.

Three months after Harry settled in, and following thorough investigations, Andrew, Bernard, and Carlton faced disciplinary hearings for their respective machinations and the issues everyone had raised against the others in the run-up to the intended promotion.

All three had breached company policy and were exited from the organisation and ironically having provided clear succession plans.

Management had an easy time replacing all three.

It is quite clear from the story that BMsm was at work. Senior management looked at the long term interests of the business and overruled the short term intentions of the three potential deputies.

There are times too when the small mind succeeds in carrying the day. Of course in such cases, the accompanying disasters follow suit but for now, let us hold it there.

Chapter 2 Models that explain BMsm

Let us begin with the attitude window.

One of the concepts used in the attitude window is scarcity and abundance mentalities. This is credited to Stephen Covey in his book Principle-Centered Leadership.

He opines that "an abundance mentality is that there is plenty out there for everyone. This abundance mentality flows out of a deep sense of personal worth and security.

It results in sharing recognition, profits, and responsibility. It opens up creative new options and alternatives. It turns personal joy and fulfillment outward. It recognizes unlimited possibilities for positive interaction growth and development."

He continues to say that "most people are deeply scripted in the scarcity mentality. They see life as a finite pie: if someone gets a big piece of the pie, it means less for everybody else.

It's a zero-sum paradigm of life. People with a scarcity mentality have a hard time sharing recognition, credit, power, or profit. They also have a tough time being genuinely happy for the success of other people-even, and sometimes especially, members of their own family or close friends and associates." I could not have put it any better.

The attitude window has four quadrants like it is here below.

	Negative attitude	Positive attitude
Big Mind	Q4	Q3
Small Mind	Q1	Q2

For our purposes, it will not all fit in one page and we shall, therefore, have it split in two. The upper half and lower half but we will bear in mind its complete picture as a four-quadrant object.

Big mind	Q4	Q3
	1-Selfishly Selects solutions 2-Switches from long to short term to suit their situation. 3- Masks rubble rousing 4-Bends rules sometimes 5-Can switch from abundance mentality to a scarcity mentality 6-May not fully forgive 7- Hides emotions 8-A flag in the wind when in a mixed group of big and small minds may or may not be reliable	1-Solution based 2-Long term focus 3-Avoids or manages the trouble 4-Stickler for rules but positively flexible as well. 5-An abundance mentality 6-Forgiving 7-Controls emotions 8-Dependable

	Q1	Q2
Small mind	1-No solutions or selfish solutions. 2-Negatively Short term 3- trouble maker 4-seeks to avoid rules given a chance 5-Scarcity mentality 5-Short cuts 6-Vengeance 7-Emotional 8- Unreliable	1- Will not provide but will accept solutions from others. 2- Neutral to long or short term focus 3- Not a trouble maker 4- Will follow rules 5-Neutral to scarcity or abundant mentality 6-A flag in the wind when mixed with small and big minds. May or may not forgive 7. emotional indifference 8-Dependable on small tasks
	Negative attitude	Positive attitude

It is quite clear that quadrant 3 is the ideal place to be in the attitude window. Unfortunately, nearly everybody alive today has a bit of all four quadrants. You do not need to be an expert to figure out someone's attitude and place in the attitude window.

First impressions may mask the true identity of a person but when you work closely with someone or live with them, their attitude becomes apparent to you.

Second is the BAST or STAB assessment.

BAST is an acronym for Big, Average, Small and Tiny.

If we fuse this with the attitude window, then Big and Average occupy the big mind quadrants and Small and Tiny occupy the small mind quadrants. Big and small both occupy the positive attitude quadrants while Average and Tiny occupy the negative attitude quadrants. So when merged, in the window it looks like this.

	A Q4	Q3 B
Big mind	1-Selfishly Selects solutions 2-Switches from long to short term to suit their situation. 3- Masks rubble rousing 4-Bends rules sometimes 5-Can switch from abundance mentality to a scarcity mentality 6-May not fully forgive 7- Hides emotions 8-A flag in the wind when in a mixed group of big and small minds may or may not be reliable	1-Solution based 2-Long term focus 3-Avoids or manages trouble 4-Stickler for rules but positively flexible as well. 5-An abundance mentality 6-Forgiving 7-Controls emotions 8-Dependable

	T Q1	Q2 S
Small mind	1-No solutions or selfish solutions. 2-Negatively Short term 3- trouble maker 4-seeks to avoid rules given a chance 5-Scarcity mentality 5-Short cuts 6-Vengeance 7-Emotional 8- Unreliable	1- Will not provide but will accept solutions from others. 2- Neutral to long or short term focus 3- Not a trouble maker 4- Will follow rules 5-Neutral to scarcity or abundant mentality 6-A flag in the wind when mixed with small and big minds. May or may not forgive 7. emotional indifference 8-Dependable on small tasks
	Negative attitude	Positive attitude

If we use BAST in another way as demonstrated here below, we can map out the different characters around us.

Let us also bring in the two situations that most people respond. We refer to them as Adapted behaviour and Natural behaviour. Adapted behaviour is displayed by someone in a controlled environment. A controlled environment is where the rules are set for someone to follow such as at work, place of worship or at a formal meeting.

Natural behaviour is displayed by someone in an environment where he or she has a high level or some level of control with the rules and norms. This will include the home or informal settings elsewhere.

We shall proceed to map out the natural and adapted behaviours of someone we shall call Beatrice.

Beatrice's Natural behaviour   Beatrice's Adapted behaviour

B	A	S	T
	1		
(2)			
		3	
	4		
			(5)
		(6)	
			7
		(8)	

B	A	S	T
1			
(2)			
	3		
4			
			(5)
		(6)	
		7	
		(8)	

From the above tables and graphs, Beatrice's behaviour is reasonably stable in both environments. Four elements are the same in both environments and those that vary are not too far from each other.

Such variations are expected of a stable character and will not change much for many people.

For others, the two behaviours are very distant and could be telling of serious problems either at home or in the workplace.

The variables as enumerated in the attitude window will not play out in exactly the same way when subjected to different environments.

This addition to the models of BMsm may create confusion or further complicate our reading of the subject matter for this book but please digest it slowly. It will make sense as we progress to the other chapters.

To create a contrast, we have provided a second example for a man named Paul. This particular example will aid us to appreciate that we are as diverse as our population out there.

It will also help us to understand that we all have different circumstances when facing our daily challenges be they at home or at work.

Paul's Natural behaviour

Paul's Adapted behaviour

B	A	S	T
1			
2			
3			
	4		
5			
6			
7			
8			

B	A	S	T
		1	
		2	
			3
			4
		5	
		6	
			7
			8

Paul's behaviours are the exact opposite. At work, he seems very collected and consistently big mind. At home, he is consistently small mind. So he could be enjoying his work in the office and undergoing a non-fulfilling life at home.

The office has a high-level commitment and the home front has little if any. Maybe Paul is drinking a lot and only gets home to sleep and prepare for the next day at work.

This second example demonstrates that BMsm can be dependent on environmental settings and we may, therefore, misread the true person.

Thirdly, let us clash the four characters base on the attitude window.

We shall look at the possible outcomes of conflicts between the following people.

1. Big Mind versus Big Mind
2. Big Mind versus Small Mind
3. Small Mind versus Big Mind
4. Small Mind versus Small Mind

Big Mind versus Big Mind conflict

If two Big minds are on opposing sides fighting over a scarce resource, they will both articulate their positions with absolute clarity and will use all logical approaches within their power to convince the other to accept their point of view.

For as long as the conversation remains between the two of them, they will remain in the big mind zone and square it out amicably.

But if in the process, one looks down upon the other or is joined by a small mind, the conversation may degenerate because any of the small mind elements have the ability if not resisted, to pull one down from Big Mind mode to small mind mode.

If the adapted behaviour is big mind and the natural behaviour is small mind for one of the protagonists and the other is solidly big mind both ways, then the conflict still has the hope of reaching a solution.

This is because big mind mode is a solution based mode and at least one person sees it that way.

All in all a Big Mind to Big Mind conflict is expected to be settled amicably.

Big Mind versus Small mind conflict.

This is one that is triggered by the Big mind and differs from Small mind versus Big mind.

In this kind of scenario, the big mind is selfless and has an abundance mentality. This person would be getting into a conflict perhaps to solve a real problem that will benefit both parties.

Under such circumstances, the Big mind will drive the process and carefully navigate the sensitive edges until a reasonable solution is attained. The big mind may even allow the small mind time off to reflect on the challenge at hand and then continue after a while.

Small mind versus Big mind.

This kind of conflict can take one of three forms. The first may go in the manner that the one of Big Mind versus Small mind went in the scenario above.

The second and most likely way is the small mind holds their ground and prolongs the conflict unnecessarily. The small mind may force his way especially if he has authority over the Big mind.

The conflict may not reach a logical conclusion but the Big mind most likely will opt to end it now and live to fight it out another day.

The third option might have the situation degenerating into a Small Mind affair. The small mind might trigger the big mind to collapse into small mind mode and worsen the situation.

The remotest possibilities from either the natural or adapted behaviour might just come alive and the true colours of an otherwise calm character come out and in a manner that the instigator was not expecting.

Small mind versus Small mind

This conflict will have many possible outcomes but one thing is for sure. Small mind mode provides no solutions but plenty of trouble. The conflict will go on and may get physical.

This kind of conflict may be resolved if a Big mind intervenes but also, it just may worsen things if one senses unfairness.

Egos come on the way of reason and emotions will surely run high and take away any possibility of a truce.

There are times when two small minds may find a solution. This is when one of them comes to his senses and convinces the other that they are both bigger than their source of conflict.

Ridicule can help get them out of small mind mode. If younger people or juniors are within the environment of conflict, they may be the motivation that restores sanity as it is embarrassing to act smaller than those viewed as smaller in every sense.

We have two other situations not dealt with yet but are important, the impact of the average mind. The average mind is what is between the big and the small mind. First, in the attitude window, negativity makes the Big mind act average. Secondly, positivity makes the small mind act average too.

From Big to average is a negative development but from small to average, is seemingly positive development.

The problem is that average has elements of negativity and is a convenient bridge through which negativity finds its way to and from Big to small.

Let the state of being an average mind never be confused for being the go-between when seeking a lasting solution between a small mind and a big mind. Average actually adulterates both big and small and can create confusion. So for our purposes, we shall treat the average mind as a small mind.

Chapter 3 Small mind triggers

In order to tame small mind mode, we must understand what triggers that state of the mind. In the book "How to Undo Life's Airlocks" now renamed "Tearless Living", I observed at the time I wrote it a basic truth about mindset.

I concluded that "mindset, regardless of where one is will always return consistent results that are commensurate to that mind." And be it adapted or natural behaviour.

This means that if you are big minded your mindset will return results consistent with that state no matter where you are. The same applies to the small mind.

The above observation on consistency holds true for the small mind that never solves problems. Let us see what locks the mind to consistently return unwarranted results.

We will not exhaust the causes but some of the triggers include the following.

First, past experiences account for many of those situations that, either activate or invigorate the small mind. If you come across someone from long ago whom you have had a nasty experience with as a result of their actions, the small mind in hibernation may awake to map out a revenge mission. Remember that revenge is a small mind specialty.

It is even worse if the cause of the pain is still promoted by the offending party. The misfortune of losing a sweetheart to someone else may be so deep-seated in the mind of the offended party that it may cause them to avoid the other party, say at a school reunion.

Now things may get physical if the same person openly sends overtures to his past victim's present sweetheart.

There is also the kind of past experience that is indirect but nonetheless triggers the small mind.

If one party comes from a family that has caused pain to another family, and perhaps some generations after the original act, his or her presence may still have the kind of potency that triggers revenge instincts on behalf of the offended clan.

Also, you may be innocent, but your resemblance to an offending party may make an affected party to hate you. Hate is a small mind specialty. It is enough to trigger negative emotional energy.

Or, you could just talk like someone else or walk like them. An attribute that you share with someone else may remind the offended person of the bad experience and because you are the functional representation of the small-mind activating thought, you may just find yourself in trouble.

Second, the availability or the lack of resources may activate the small mind. One may not know how to handle the abundance of resources while another may not know any better ways of overcoming the scarcity of resources.

Lack of money may cause someone to steal in order to solve the urgent demands of life. Theft is a small mind action. Kleptomania is very much a small mind disease. Denying others what is rightfully theirs is small mind activity.

Lack of basic needs as in Maslow's hierarchy of needs- shelter, food, clothing, sex, and sanitation may cause theft, rape or other forms of compensatory mechanisms all in an effort to solve the short term needs. A short term state is squarely in the small mind's jurisdiction.

On the other hand, when one is overcome by the abundance of wealth, they may get confused and get wasteful. This may be so in instances where sudden wealth is involved. The inexperienced mind may have no long term plan. Lack of such a plan is a small mind indicator.

Another trigger is a sense or realization of being mentally or physically weaker than peers. A feeling of subservience or being left behind by others is never a good one. The big mind may plot out a long term plan to overcome the situation, but the small mind will want a shortcut.

Throughout our lives, we get to those moments that clearly make us feel lost or totally out of our depth. It could be at a new job or assignment, or a new social setting that we are counting on for a better living. Our reaction to such changes will either be big or small mind.

Small mind mode in its typical impatient style, will invite panic mode. Panic mode is a small mind attribute. Panic occurs when no known road map is available.

To sum it all up, a scarcity mentality is a key driver and has the master key to opening the door into the small mind's world. It is not difficult to spot someone of this undesirable mentality.

Chapter 4 Manifestations of the small mind

The small mind mode has a devastating impact on both the individual and the organisation. An organisation full of small heads will struggle to remain relevant in the market place and will more often than not collapse or if it survives, becomes the living example of how not to work.

The manifestations of the small mind in any environment has a lot to do with the heavy presence of negative energy. The results of the small mind are well known but we must watch out for its appearances.

First, whenever small mind mode is switched on, one can never be productive or be of any good use to important activity.

For instance, if you are part of a strategic team meeting and suddenly a small mind trigger activates your small mind, you will not be of any use to that meeting.

Let me give you some examples to think about.

1. If at this meeting, a beautiful woman or very handsome man walks into the room and a member of the attracted gender gets taken away by the thought of having that person for his or herself, then immediately, small mind mode checks in.

Short term-ness activates and is now in total contradiction of the long term nature of the strategic planning meeting.

At best, the small minded person will pretend to follow proceedings but in actual sense is very far away from the room mentally. It is most noticeable when the usually very active participants in the room go mute.

2. If someone that one of the participants present has had a nasty encounter with, as we saw in chapter three, walked in or was referred to in this meeting, this may trigger small mind mode in the offended participant.

Moving forward, they will struggle to be useful in a forum otherwise set for discussing long term objectives.

3. If in this meeting, chauvinism prevails over reason, for instance, someone gets discriminated against on the basis of gender, religion, race, political affiliation or tribe. When stereotypes guide proceedings and facts are left out of the conversations, then small mind mode is in full bloom.

A promotion earned using small mind tactics has no solid foundation. The key term here is tactics and not strategy. Tactics are associated with the short term yet, a promotion is meant to address a long term strategic objective of the organisation or whatever entity is in question. Could be that the boss got favours in kind from the promoted staffer but when the boss exits the scene, the promoted person may find themselves in rough waters.

To compensate for the undeserved promotion, the occupant of the position will make very many compromises and offer several olive branches to please the offended members of the team.

Whenever you see a boss giving too many concessions, think twice about why this is happening. Do not mistake an open management style also for a manifestation of the works of a small mind.

Arrogance is a small mind manifestation. It most often is compensation for confidence. When something was done right, one would exude confidence but where the small mind crafted something, arrogance manifests.

Unwarranted competition is a small mind display. Oftentimes on the road, you find a driver in top speed chasing after a car that was purposely built for speed.

Not that his car cannot move fast, but the motivation is just to prove a point, that he can drive fast as well. An ambulance at work is self-explanatory but a regular type car behaving like an ambulance only to pull over to a parking slot and then the driver just walks slowly thereafter to wherever he was going to, is very telling of a huge ego.

The acronym PhD is many times associated with great academic achievements but it has another meaning too. To the small mind, PhD stands for Pull him or her down. To the big mind, PhD denotes, pat him or her for the good deeds. So one gives credit where it is due and another one attempts to wipe it out altogether.

The small mind has its indelible signature. For a small mind to look good, someone else must look bad. This is when the small mind employs all its tools including deceit, jealousy, manipulation and other pain inducers from its bag of implements.

Often times when just one person shines and everyone else is looking bad, check again, you will find that a small mind worked overtime.

Most times, the small mind acts for maximum impact and especially when all the big guns are in town. A diligent employee can be made to look mediocre through sabotage.

Remember that for someone to look good, someone else must look bad according to the small mind.

The small mind also cannot face up to a challenge that it has caused. For example, when a small mind is indebted to someone else, and the repayment date has reached or passed, it will tend to hide, run away or ignore his lender.

The big mind would at least face the lender and seek an alternative date after explaining the situation out. The big mind finds solutions while the small mind creates problems.

Let us end this on a positive note with the story below that also serves as a soft landing into chapter 5.

James works for a leading financial institution at a rural county headquarters. As branch manager, James is respected within the local county leadership circles. The Governor invites him alongside peers for national holiday celebrations as well as important leadership forums.

At work, James's branch frequently receives head office commendations for meeting or exceeding set objectives. The branch team is very motivated and solidly behind their leader.

It has been five years since James got appointed to the position and he has built a beautiful home for his family. Mrs. James is the leader of the elite women's investment group in town. They have an impressive portfolio of property and business activities and are now the envy of many.

James has also amassed a respectable amount of wealth together with friends at his private members' club. Life is at its best and everyone wants this to continue forever.

The company board has identified James as the ideal replacement for a senior manager who is exiting the business at the headquarters in downtown Nairobi. Senior management has also identified a suitable replacement at the branch.

After a month, James finds himself in the city. Initially, the jitters within the family nearly caused James to resign because they had figured out that the absence of the job would not make a noticeable dent to their lives, after all, they were doing well already.

The new position came with perks not enjoyed before, the company paid school fees for all the kids in top end schools, a fully paid house in the leafy suburbs, a fitting car and many other trappings that came with the new assignment.

To make up for his absence from his personal business activities, James promoted a confidant to supervise all his investments and all goes well.

At the headquarters, things turn out differently, the colleagues who often talked well with James while at the branch; have all gone cold on him now that they work from the same building.

The position he now holds was in the hands of someone else who had acted for two months and all indications were that he was destined for the coveted position. John, Knew that he had done well and could not understand why he missed the job.

Most staffers were sympathetic with John's situation and the lines were clearly drawn. It was a fight between born towns and rural boys.

Things are also different. There are no more invitations to national celebrations and members at his new club don't seem to have time for him. His ideas don't fit into the prevailing tempo. It is a whole new ball game for James.

The children are unhappy with the new school experience. They are picked on and laughed at every time they speak. They now realize that they have heavy accents laced with mother tongue interference.

Mrs. James is also not getting along well with the neighbours, the new church group and those in her new circles. From being the leader back at the rural county to now being a nobody, is hard to swallow.

Back at the house, everyone is frustrated and missing their previous life. They are all at wit's end and everyone pleads with

James to take them back home but James sees things differently.

He tells his family to view the new challenges positively. "We cannot impose our ways on people with set ways and especially when we are the new people around." He asked everyone to tone down and agree to be taught into new ways of life in the city. "Ask your classmates to show you what you need to do to fit in. don't take offense."

At the office, James stayed calm and slowly won his way into the hearts of his colleagues. He knew that he had to remain in big mind state to overcome the small minds around him. He quietly influenced management's decision to move John to another department and gave equal growth opportunities to everyone in his department.

By the end of the school term, the kids had several friends requesting for a sleepover at James's house. They had sharpened their accents and had blended in very well. Mrs. James was now rising in importance within the new circles and life began to normalize.

Within three years, the board appointed James to the Managing Director's position and moving forward, all went well till James retired from the company.

Remember that "mindset, regardless of where one is will always return consistent results that are commensurate to that mind."

James was able to read through the schematics of the small minds in the office and kept his long term success objective alive. He successfully guided his family to have a positive outlook even when faced by uncomfortable challenges. That is what a big mind does anywhere anytime.

Chapter 5 Nourishing the big mind and starving the small mind

Suppose you are driving from Nairobi to Nakuru some 150 kilometers away and you are tuned to your favourite FM radio station. As you drive past the city limits, your reception goes hazy and you are forced to change the signal frequency.

So at the beginning of your journey, it could have been 101 FM, at the next point it may have been 89.4 FM and at a third point, you may have switched it to 74.3 FM. All these you did to keep listening to your favourite station.

That is what happens to us as we face our challenges. We must keep searching for our true north. A similar experience confronts pilots in turbulent weather.

The plane changes course because strong winds push it to a new direction but the pilot must keep finding the planned course in order to avoid accidents with oncoming planes and to stick within acceptable paths with authorities of the territories that the plane is overflying.

The big mind acts in the same way. If we stop the tuning or reclaiming the correct path, then surely the small mind will take over for life abhors a vacuum.

The onus of remaining firmly fixed in big mind mode is ours as individuals.

Life will throw at us varying situation but it is entirely upon us to recalibrate ourselves back to big mind territory.

Here is a harsh reality. 80% of the situations that you face won't go according to the script. 20 % may. The world will not simply cooperate with us so that we have it easy.

This statistic should, therefore, make us very aware that falling into small mind zone is easier than staying firmly in the big mind zone because the world has a bigger say in what we face.

To overcome this, we must get used to the mind switch concept. If you are at home or at work, you may turn on or switch on the lights or the computer, so that you can work or see things better.

Likewise, when confronted by any situation, you must tell yourself that I am on big mind mode or let me switch on to big mind mode. This enables you to avoid panic mode. It keeps you on long term mode and planning mode or solutions mode.

Tell yourself in your mind "I refuse to switch to small mind mode."

When someone you had bad experiences with shows up or when someone you regard as a small mind has to be in your presence, remind yourself that being in Big mind mode is the ideal situation. That way, irritants don't hold sway on your mood anymore.

Find time to be around big-minded people for highly engaging debates and discussion. An exchange of ideas with such people serves to remind you of the sweetness of being big minded.

As with anything in life, practice makes perfect. The more you practice the better you get at being in big mind territory.

There is the temptation of accomplishing many things over a relatively short space of time and at such moments little short term goals may give one a high sense of success. When this is repeated too often, one may drift focus to small mind territory.

It is therefore very important to work with the mind switch concept so that you are always reminding yourself that you are switched on for big mind activity.

If you are a confessed small mind and making amends to migrate to big mind territory, you will struggle with your past.

Remember that because you lack big mind experience in seeking solutions when a challenging situation emerges, you will find that your lack of big territory experience, will summon your default mode of the familiar small mind actions.

This is your opportunity to starve the small mind mode of any further involvement in your life. It won't be easy as it comes so naturally yet, you want to get it out of your system.

When you are in between the full transition from a small mind to big mind zone, inevitably, you will accomplish some small mind tasks and then remember that you must revert to your desired big mind.

During such times, remember that when your next task is a big mind zone type, you will find it hard to summon all the focus needed to attain the task at hand. You must, therefore, take a little break to allow the big mind's switch to fully activate.

One of the most effective ways of developing a new habit is to review what has happened on a daily basis. It is easier while things are still fresh to list down all the tasks or challenges of the day.

What doesn't get measured doesn't get done. You must measure yourself as honestly as possible and compare the statistics with the previous days.

This approach increases your self-awareness and enables you to have a target to work with.

To starve a habit, it means that you must deny it of the food that allows it to thrive. It is therefore imperative that you make a list of all the negative aspects that keep you on the small-minded side of life.

With your list, work on eliminating their recurrence by reviewing your activities daily.

Crop off associates who keep your small mind mode nourished. It looks tough but it is inevitable. You will never see things long term when your environment is very much a short term one.

It is about your improvement and not everyone's so, for now, focus on yourself. When they see your positive changes, you will be the example that encourages desired change in them too.

Chapter 6 Get into the small mind to tame it

Never condemn the small mind unheard. Call it dalliance, but there are times when it is necessary to wade into small mind territory, but only for the sake of understanding it when in big mind territory.

Normally, the big mind is not naïve to the machinations of the small mind. In fact when mama said "don't talk to strangers" she was inducting you into the world of several small minds that can harm you.

The small mind is often dangerous to itself and those around it. When it harbours revenge missions on big minders for whatever reasons, then it is better to be safe than sorry

You are partly a big mind courtesy of the need to distinguish yourself from the small mind and partly because you may have one such mind in the past. The truth is, your mind is no virgin to the workings of the small mind.

It is crucial to seek to know what happens in the small mind in order to better manage its wasteful activities. This is why responsible governments research on crime trends and seek to understand the triggers then, address them conclusively.

At the personal level, the workings of the small mind are crucial to your plans because the adversity factor influences all plans. There is always a small mind here and there that is hell-bent on puncturing your activities. The small mind will make you work overtime on otherwise easily achievable goals.

In many situations in life, the small mind will throw a spanner in the works and we must factor this in and deal with it.

So, when you have completed your plan, get to the stage that asks what if?

Ask yourself what can the small mind do to spoil your intended end game? Sometimes, get the views of a safer small mind for it takes a thief to catch a thief.

Smart managers, sometimes invite their colleagues to a meeting disguised as an important planning session, just to pick the thoughts of the small minds within, then work out ways of handling them before they act.

The small mind, when guided to big mind territory, can be of use to the big mind when seeking to find solutions to defeat the small mind's actions and thoughts.

For instance, when you have an important event coming up, it is useful to brainstorm together on what can go wrong. The small mind when motivated positively, will disclose all the bad things that can happen. It is like how you train a sniffer dog to catch the bad guys.

Getting into the mind of the small minds to better understand them is no excuse to become a small mind yourself. Temptations are conceived in the small mind and also executed in the same mode. We do not need to elaborate anything here.

Let us appreciate the big mind at work through a small mind to attain the desired end in the story below.

Somewhere in Africa, there was this village where it was very prestigious to own a dog. Breeds never mattered as they were all mixed cross mongrels. The enterprising fellows in this village saw the business opportunity and created a dog market.

On a certain day of every week, people came with dogs to sell and there were many buyers. Soon enough, people in the surrounding villages began to complain about their lost dogs. Search teams were instituted but all in vain.

One day, a rich villager awoke to empty kennels. He had diligently fed and cared well for his dogs. They were very loyal to him but on that night that they went missing, they gave away no clue, not even the customary barking when strange things came close by.

It was painful as these were pure breed dogs.

He was now a new addition to the growing statistics of lost dogs' owners. And because he had the resources, this rich villager decided to investigate the menace.

He and a team of like-minded people quietly profiled all the potential suspects in the dog trade and called for a meeting to support youth groups in the area.

With high unemployment rates, it made sense to get the youth organized into manageable teams matched up with specific opportunities that they could profit from.

One group looked unique; they never revealed the kind of business venture that they wanted the rich man to help them out with. They promised to come back with a concrete plan in two weeks' time when all the rest were required to report progress.

Coincidentally, the profile of the potential suspects compiled earlier by the like-minded wise men matched with the members of this secretive group of eight members.

Every group was assigned a mentor from amongst the wise and more successful men and women in the village. The one assigned to the secretive group had a hard time trying to help them figure out what to do.

They seemed satisfied with life and were visibly better dressed daily when compared to peers. The mentor overheard one of them talking to someone on the phone. The conversation was about the delivery of some cargo at night. The pick-up truck for the job was to come from a town forty miles away.

As the conversation went on, it became clearer to the mentor that this group of smartly dressed youth was in the dog trade.

The mentor informed the bigger group of mentors and elaborate plans were set in motion. That material night, all the other youth in the other groups secretly worked with the mentors to catch them red-handed but something gave the plan away.

The suspects never did anything and lay low for two weeks as they monitored the situation.

At the next meeting, the rich villager offered any youth able to get him three good dogs the equivalent of USD 1,000. In the village, that was a lot of money and everyone went out of their way to find the desired type of dogs.

One of the members of the odd group approached the rich man and asked him for his pick-up as he had found three dogs that met his guidelines. The rich man yielded but on condition that his driver was in charge of the vehicle.

They got the dogs and on close examination, they were the lost dogs. The odd group member sort assurances on his identity from the rich man and his driver after pocketing the USD 1,000.

Next, the rich man asked his new accomplice how the dog trade was done and he got a blow by blow account of it. He also disclosed when and what time the next consignment was to be delivered. This time around, the gang was nabbed and locked up.

The collaborator had cleverly gone to visit a sick uncle in the city some 200 miles away. On his return, he paid them a visit in prison to personally establish exactly what happened.

It surely got a thief to catch a thief.

Let us also consider some additional things about the small mind.

1. **The small mind's wasteful time freezing technique.**

Begrudging is a small mind occupation. When you begrudge someone, it affects you more than it does to your target. You freeze time and you are trapped in a sorry state for as long as the grudge is never let go.

A coping mechanism is what you need most.

You must accept that what has happened has happened. Then you must accept that the task of coming out of the situation is your responsibility and not your source of grief.

You must then find a formula to restore yourself. You must anchor your recovery to your long term objectives because in this kind of situations, the temptation to be short term minded is very strong.

You can forgive and move on but never forget that the small mind can repeat the pain causing act.

So also have a plan to deal with it if it happens again, something akin to a bank's disaster preparedness plan in its business continuity strategy should the building burn down or the systems fail when required.

2. The Small mind deception.

The small mind shares many attributes with the big mind. They are both, therefore, they both know how and what it means to relate with other humans.

The only difference here is that one is genuine and the other is disguised in their interactions with others.

The small mind observes well and can clearly see that when one behaves like a big mind, they attract instant admiration and respect from others around them.

The small mind is very calculating and the natural instinct to survive any situation drives it to align with widely accepted norms. This realisation is the reason that many people mask their true identities as small minds.

Dig this. A job vacancy is announced and several people submit their applications. Four people get shortlisted.

All four candidates give a good account of themselves and the interviewing panel is spoilt for choice.

The truth is, three candidates were dishonest with their real experiences and personalities. One candidate said it as it was.

The interviewers ranked the honest one last of the four, but procedures dictated that the four get subjected to a background expert's assessment.

The results were shocking. The top-ranked candidates had obvious flows in their accounts of who they actually were and what they had really accomplished.

Several time gaps between jobs had been carefully covered up by extending in their resumes the actual times worked.

The initially lowest ranked candidate got the job and proceeded to diligently execute his duties.

The three unsuccessful candidates had rehearsed all possible scenarios and beat the interviewers to it. They acted like big minds when in actual fact, they were small minds.

Mimicking the big mind may get you places but it won't change your true nature.

It is, for this reason, that big minds deliberately slow down some processes.

The diligence is a very crucial big mind exercise. Courtship before marriage is one such thing that uncovers any short term natured personality traits in someone you need to decide on in the long term sense.

The small mind deception is an act of survival and not a desire to upgrade from small to big mind. Unfortunately, many promising relationships, organisations or teams carry undeserving people who only serve to pull down everyone.

The adapted behaviours of some small minds get them through the doors that matter but their natural behaviours over time, take over and the true colours get to full bloom when it is too late.

They have fully achieved their intended purpose and are ready to move on to the next station in life, and all because they mimicked the big mind.

3. The compounding effect on life

Both big mind and small mind activities intrinsically have a compounding effect.

If you stay on the big mind side of life both in letter and spirit, your positive influence on all around you becomes evident and many people get naturally attracted to your magnetic pull.

Life begins to feel easier because you no longer struggle with trust as you are consistent and worthy of everyone's trust.

On the other hand, when you are a small mind major, the compounding effect only serves to make things harder and out of reach.

It may take longer to acknowledge this state of affairs because misery loves company and the more things compound on you, the more they feel normal because you have sympathisers and empathisers in equal measure who get you to think that life is a lot like it is now.

The small mind locks you into a position that mirrors the consistency of the big mind but in effect a state that ensures that you are left behind by the prevailing fundamentals.

You may find yourself part of a business association or other form of grouping that is meant to benefit you from the economies of scale.

But in reality, it only blindness you further from actually seeking better fitting alternatives such as gainful employment that would earn you more than what you get from marking time miserably.

The small mind has a way of justifying wasteful situations by mimicking the big mind.

Any consistent activity that yields little over an extended period of time and without justification, is a small mind's gimmick of progress. Subscribers beware.

Chapter 7 how BMsm affects the rites of passage at work

In life, we know of the four rites of passage-Birth, initiation to adulthood, marriage, and death. Each of these stages has elaborate ceremonies.

The same can be said of the workplace; we have the day of employment, confirmation, promotion, transfer, and exit by choice, by the employer's choice or by death.

When one gets employed, his or her biggest milestone is to successfully complete the probation period and get their employment status confirmed.

One can choose to flow with the many short term offers and destructions or stick to the long term objectives and get fully aligned to what is expected of them.

The workplace for many of us is where we go to in order to achieve long term objectives that include leading a quality life.

When small mind mode takes centre stage, it becomes difficult to attain any of our set objectives.Let us not dwell too much on the probation period. The next stage is crucial in our personal development.

We now have the job and all expectations clearly articulated and you are busy doing your job.As with most places, there is the official organogram and the job grades and associated trappings clearly spelled out and then there is the political map not too obviously conspicuous.

When such a situation exists, many people align to the political map where camps exist for the expediency of the powers that be.

Let me clarify that there is positive politicking and negative politicking. One belongs to the long term side of things and the other belongs to the short term side of things.

When one uses his or her track record to argue for additional resources in order to accomplish company tasks, then that is a positive politicking move.

When someone manipulates the system to get the undue advantage over others so as to look good when the rest are made to look bad, that is negative politicking.

If you find yourself a pawn in the negative political chess board, then be very afraid because your long term interests and the short term interests of your senior are at a crossroads.

After you have served the purposes of aiding in inflicting pain at colleagues, those of a similar persuasion may exact revenge when favourable conditions prevail. The workplace many times is a swamp. It has the insects, the cold-blooded alligators and all manner of filthy animals.

The workplace is the official place for perfecting adapted behaviour and what you see is not always what you get because people are not showing their true colours.

What may pass for a gentleman in the office may actually be a terror at home and on occasion and particularly when revenge is in the air, the natural behaviour may get displayed momentarily.

The workplace is where one must be very cautious of either operating as a small mind or falling victim to the machinations of small minds.

How you work determines which rite of passage comes first. Will it be the promotion or the exit? Will it be a forced transfer or an unwarranted elevation?

Do you report to a Manager or a Prime Minister? Or precisely a Professional or a politician in the workplace?

Failure to get the balance right only ensures that you do not fulfill your purpose in the organisation and possibly you are on your way out.

Chapter 8 Examples of big mind leadership

Let us examine some big mind leaders and how they navigated small mind situations.

1. Nelson Mandela and the apartheid regime.

The act of not exacting revenge on individuals in the apartheid administrations in South Africa can only be viewed as big mind actions.

Nelson Mandela had suffered mentally, physically and emotionally. He had obviously lost a big part of his productive life to prison time.

Later, he divorced his wife because they had drifted apart largely due to his incarceration.

As president, he had the power through the popular will of the people to avenge for his mistreatment but for him, the future of his people was more important to personal suffering.

He steered the nation to what lay ahead and away from a divisive past. After serving one term, he handed power to his successor and moved on. Many African leaders of his time could not match up to this big mind actions.

2. Lee Kuan Yew – founding father of Singapore

When he resolved to transform Singapore from a far-flung outpost in the high seas to a modern first world country within one generation, many thought that it was not possible.

Some people bore the brunt of his unwavering initiatives. He was more benevolent than selfishly ruthless even when it seemingly made no sense in the early days.

Like many leaders, he had the choice and opportunity to line his pockets by looting his county's coffers, but instead, he chose to run the country in a pragmatic and progressive manner.

Today, Singaporeans enjoy some of the best of most things including a good quality lifestyle thanks to Lee Kwan Yew.

3. King Solomon and the two mothers

When two mothers were brought before the king, one mother had carelessly slept on her child to death.

The other mother was careful and nursed her child well.

On realizing that she had killed her own child, the woman decided to claim the other child who was alive and this troubling situation was taken before King Solomon to make a ruling.

When the king ordered that the living child be cut in two so that each mother would have a piece of it, the real mother cried out to the king and pleaded that it was better to give the child away to the other woman. To her, the long term welfare of the child was more important to what was about to happen.

Her plea touched the king who was able to then establish that the pleading mother was indeed the real mother of the child. She was handed her child and she went home a happy woman.

The big mind cares more about life.

4. The new Prime Minister of Ethiopia (2018) Abiy Ahmed

Ethiopia is the second most populous country in Africa and has internal dynamics that need a careful mind.

When the new Prime Minister assumed power, He found a near-impossible situation to manage. The majority tribe by a wide margin was unhappy with the treatment meted out on them by the ruling class.

Pent up anger was daringly manifesting in protests and deadly demonstration that caught the world's attention.

His predecessors had either been at war with or sustained the hostilities with neighbouring Eritrea which had broken away from Ethiopia through self-determination. This made Ethiopia landlocked and caused it to seek alternative port routes through other countries.

During the war, brother went against brother for many in the two countries are related by blood.

So within his first few days in office, the Prime Minister apologized to the Oromo people for the atrocities meted out on them by past regimes.

This had a disarming effect in the hearts of the Oromo and the tensions that were building up diffused as their side of the story finally had some caring enough to listen.

He then got Eritrea on the talking table and settled outstanding issues and fully restored diplomatic ties. The whole world watched in disbelief as this happened.

He then went out to strengthen ties with all neighbouring countries and got his country focused on their development agenda.

Much as for a long time now, Ethiopia has enjoyed a sustained high growth rate, the distribution of the benefits will now be more inclusive and in turn, the growth trajectory will reflect the new momentum.

It is only big mind thinking that can rise above oppression, revenge and sectarian chauvinism to get the impossible to possible heights.

5. Mwai Kibaki, Kenya's 3rd President (2003 -2013)

When he came to power, he immediately fulfilled his free primary school education pledge against a backdrop of many nay Sayers.

At an interview in the early days of the Kibaki regime, Former US President Bill Clinton, when interviewed was asked about whom he would want to visit at the world stage, and after a thoughtful pause said, "the new President of Kenya. He scrapped school fees and a million more kids turned up in schools."

Today those kids are nearly half of Kenya's population.

That was big mind leadership. President Kibaki also gave Kenya its economic blueprint dubbed vision 2030 and whose end game is to guide Kenya's transformation into a middle-income society with its citizens enjoying a good quality lifestyle by the year 2030.

A few but impact full legacies. He also never found it fit to respond to every kind of criticism leveled against him by the political class.

For him, actions spoke louder than words.

6. Cement company business is taken away.

For this example, I find that the lesson therein is more important than knowing the name of the country in question because, its citizens are undoubtedly very hard working, but were let down by elements within its national leadership.

A continental cement company in Africa completed a feasibility study in the East African region and identified a suitable location for its planned factory.

The chosen country had a seaport for easy exports and the importation of essential raw materials not locally available.

When this organisation applied to set up the ultramodern plant that promised many jobs to the locals, a senior man in government demanded a hefty bribe.

But because the works on the industrial plant had to get underway in line with the organisations long term plans, they quickly elected to move on with option 2, a landlocked country that offered better incentives and no bribes.

The big mind-action of the cement company was in its decision to exercise the second option rather than bribe or delay its plans.

Today from their new location, they are in business and have employed several locals. The small-minded rent seeker in the initial country cost the citizens a huge opportunity.

Nothing is worse than being locked up in the dungeons of poor leadership. Big mind is the way to go.

About the Author.

David Mugun is a business management consultant, speaker, and author.

This is his fifth book. The other four are indicated in the front pages of this book and are all available at Amazon.com.

He has contributed articles to magazines and newspapers including the Standard, Business daily and the East African.

David has advised and trained several organizations on strategic issues, on the back of his experience from several years of employment, spanning different industries.

He started his career in the office automation industry and has held senior positions in insurance, banking and more recently in Business education, where he was Director for Executive education at the Strathmore Business School.

David has held directorships in companies and membership-based associations in Kenya and has managed assignments all over Africa and in Europe.

He lives in Nairobi with his family.